EMMANUEL JOSEPH

Eco-Tech Couture, Style Meets Sustainability

Copyright © 2025 by Emmanuel Joseph

All rights reserved. No part of this publication may be reproduced, stored or transmitted in any form or by any means, electronic, mechanical, photocopying, recording, scanning, or otherwise without written permission from the publisher. It is illegal to copy this book, post it to a website, or distribute it by any other means without permission.

First edition

*This book was professionally typeset on Reedsy.
Find out more at reedsy.com*

Contents

1	Chapter 1: The Dawn of Eco-Tech Couture	1
2	Chapter 2: Sustainable Fabrics: From Trash to Treasure	3
3	Chapter 3: Tech-Infused Textiles	5
4	Chapter 4: Circular Fashion: The Art of Upcycling	7
5	Chapter 5: Digital Design: Innovating Sustainability	9
6	Chapter 6: The Power of Collaboration	11
7	Chapter 7: Eco-Friendly Dyeing Techniques	13
8	Chapter 8: The Rise of Slow Fashion	15
9	Chapter 9: Green Fashion Capitals	17
10	Chapter 10: Education and Advocacy	19
11	Chapter 11: Biodegradable Fashion	21
12	Chapter 12: Ethical Supply Chains	23
13	Chapter 13: Fashion for a Cause	25
14	Chapter 14: The Future of Sustainable Fashion	27
15	Chapter 15: A Global Movement	29

1

Chapter 1: The Dawn of Eco-Tech Couture

In the early 21st century, fashion was at a crossroads. The industry was battling the consequences of fast fashion and its devastating environmental impact. Enter Harper Green, a visionary designer with an unyielding passion for sustainability. Harper's journey began with a serendipitous encounter with Alex Choi, a tech guru who saw the potential of technology to revolutionize sustainable practices. Together, they embarked on a mission to meld couture with cutting-edge eco-technologies, marking the dawn of a new era.

Harper and Alex's collaboration brought about the creation of "Eco-Tech Couture," a movement that fused fashion with innovation. Their first collection, "Rebirth," showcased garments made from biodegradable fabrics and smart textiles. Each piece was not only a fashion statement but also a testament to the potential of sustainable fashion. The world took notice, and Eco-Tech Couture quickly gained a following among fashion enthusiasts and environmentalists alike.

One of their most iconic creations was the Solar Dress, a garment that harnessed solar energy to power small devices. This groundbreaking design not only reduced the wearer's carbon footprint but also demonstrated the limitless possibilities of eco-tech fashion. The Solar Dress became a symbol of the movement, inspiring designers worldwide to explore the intersection of fashion and technology.

The success of Eco-Tech Couture was not without its challenges. Harper and Alex faced skepticism from industry veterans and had to overcome numerous technical hurdles. However, their unwavering dedication and innovative spirit propelled them forward. With each collection, they pushed the boundaries of what was possible, proving that fashion could be both stylish and sustainable.

As Eco-Tech Couture continued to grow, Harper and Alex realized that their mission was more than just creating beautiful garments. They wanted to inspire a global movement towards sustainability, one that would reshape the fashion industry for generations to come. Their journey was just beginning, and the future of fashion looked brighter than ever.

2

Chapter 2: Sustainable Fabrics: From Trash to Treasure

Imagine walking down the runway, adorned in an exquisite gown spun from ocean plastics and agricultural residue. This is the magic of sustainable fabrics. Designers began to see the ocean not as a dumping ground, but as a treasure trove of untapped potential. The transformation of waste into luxurious fabrics became a testament to human ingenuity and environmental stewardship.

Take, for instance, the collaboration between environmental scientist Maya Patel and designer Jules Rivera. Maya's expertise in converting ocean waste into textile fibers combined with Jules' flair for fashion brought forth collections that were not just garments, but statements of purpose. Their pioneering work led to the creation of SeaSilk, a fabric derived from discarded fishing nets and plastic bottles.

SeaSilk quickly became a favorite among eco-conscious designers and consumers. Its soft, luxurious feel and vibrant colors made it indistinguishable from traditional silk. Fashion houses around the world began incorporating SeaSilk into their collections, turning ocean waste into high-end fashion. This innovative fabric not only reduced plastic pollution but also highlighted the potential of sustainable materials.

Another groundbreaking fabric was Agraloft, developed by scientist-turned-designer Leila Thompson. Agraloft was made from agricultural waste, such as corn husks and wheat straw, which were traditionally discarded. Leila's revolutionary process transformed these materials into a versatile fabric that could be used for both everyday wear and haute couture.

The rise of sustainable fabrics marked a significant shift in the fashion industry. Designers and consumers alike began to prioritize environmental impact over fleeting trends. The success of materials like SeaSilk and Agraloft demonstrated that fashion could be both eco-friendly and luxurious. As more designers embraced sustainable fabrics, the industry took a crucial step towards a greener future.

The journey from trash to treasure was not without its challenges. Developing sustainable fabrics required extensive research, innovation, and collaboration. However, the passion and dedication of pioneers like Maya, Jules, and Leila paved the way for a new era in fashion. Their work inspired countless others to explore the potential of sustainable materials, proving that fashion could be a force for good.

3

Chapter 3: Tech-Infused Textiles

Solar-powered jackets that charge your devices on the go, or dresses that change color based on environmental data—these are not figments of a sci-fi imagination but the reality of tech-infused textiles. Innovators like Sophia Zhang bridged the gap between science and fashion, creating garments that were as functional as they were stylish.

One of Sophia's crowning achievements was the development of LumaFiber, a fabric that stored solar energy and emitted a soft glow in low-light conditions. LumaFiber garments not only reduced the need for external lighting but also created a mesmerizing visual effect. This innovative fabric quickly gained popularity among both fashion designers and tech enthusiasts.

Sophia's work extended beyond aesthetics. She collaborated with engineers to create garments that could monitor the wearer's health, regulate body temperature, and even respond to environmental changes. These smart textiles had the potential to revolutionize not only fashion but also healthcare and emergency services.

The journey of tech-infused textiles was filled with exciting discoveries and challenges. Designers and engineers had to work together to integrate technology seamlessly into garments without compromising comfort or style. This collaboration led to the creation of multifunctional clothing that could adapt to the wearer's needs in real time.

One of the most notable collaborations was between designer Olivia Carter and engineer Max Kim. Together, they developed the Evolve Jacket, a garment that could transform its shape and color based on the wearer's environment and mood. The Evolve Jacket became a sensation, showcasing the limitless possibilities of tech-infused textiles.

As the tech-infused textiles movement continued to grow, it became clear that the future of fashion was intertwined with technology. These innovative garments not only enhanced the wearer's experience but also contributed to sustainability by reducing the need for additional resources. The potential of tech-infused textiles was limitless, and designers like Sophia, Olivia, and Max were at the forefront of this exciting revolution.

4

Chapter 4: Circular Fashion: The Art of Upcycling

In the world of fast fashion, garments were once discarded as quickly as trends changed. However, circular fashion pioneers like Emani Wilson saw discarded items as blank canvases waiting to be reborn. The art of upcycling turned fashion waste into one-of-a-kind masterpieces.

Emani's boutique became a haven for fashion enthusiasts who cherished individuality and sustainability. Each piece she created told a story of redemption and creativity, proving that beauty could indeed rise from the ashes of waste. Her collections featured garments made from vintage fabrics, old clothing, and even discarded household items.

One of Emani's most memorable creations was a stunning evening gown made entirely from discarded neckties. The gown's intricate design and vibrant colors captivated audiences and highlighted the potential of upcycled fashion. Emani's work inspired countless designers to embrace the principles of circular fashion and explore the creative possibilities of upcycling.

The rise of circular fashion marked a significant shift in consumer behavior. Shoppers began to prioritize quality and sustainability over fast fashion's disposable nature. This change was driven by a growing awareness of the environmental impact of fashion waste and the desire for unique, personalized garments.

Emani's success led to collaborations with other designers and brands, further promoting the principles of circular fashion. Together, they created collections that celebrated sustainability and creativity. These collaborations showcased the potential of upcycling and encouraged consumers to rethink their approach to fashion.

The journey of circular fashion was not without its challenges. Designers had to navigate the complexities of sourcing materials and creating cohesive collections from disparate items. However, the passion and creativity of pioneers like Emani Wilson paved the way for a new era in fashion. Their work demonstrated that fashion could be both sustainable and innovative, inspiring a global movement towards circular fashion.

5

Chapter 5: Digital Design: Innovating Sustainability

In an era where digital realms intertwine with reality, fashion found its greenest ally. Digital design revolutionized the fashion industry by reducing the need for physical samples and minimizing waste. Visionaries like Riko Tanaka spearheaded this digital transformation.

Riko's innovative approach to digital design allowed designers to create virtual prototypes and conduct virtual fashion shows, significantly reducing the industry's environmental footprint. Her work led to the development of Virtual Couture, a platform that enabled designers to experiment with new ideas without the need for physical materials.

One of Riko's most notable achievements was the creation of a virtual fashion show that garnered international attention. The show featured digital garments that could be customized and purchased by consumers, bridging the gap between virtual and physical fashion. This groundbreaking event demonstrated the potential of digital design to revolutionize the industry.

Digital design also played a crucial role in making fashion more accessible. Emerging designers could now showcase their work to a global audience without the need for expensive runway shows or physical collections. This democratization of fashion allowed for greater diversity and creativity in the industry.

As the digital design movement continued to gain momentum, it became clear that technology could be a powerful tool for sustainability. Virtual couture allowed designers to push the boundaries of creativity while minimizing their environmental impact. The success of digital design highlighted the potential of technology to transform the fashion industry for the better.

Riko's work inspired countless designers to embrace digital design and explore its possibilities. As more designers adopted virtual tools, the fashion industry took a significant step towards a more sustainable future. The journey of digital design was just beginning, and its potential to innovate sustainability was limitless.

6

Chapter 6: The Power of Collaboration

Collaboration has always been a cornerstone of innovation, and the world of eco-tech couture is no exception. Designers, scientists, and engineers came together to create groundbreaking collections that pushed the boundaries of fashion and sustainability. One such collaboration was between renowned designer Isabella Cruz and chemist Dr. Liam Chen. Together, they developed a fabric made from algae, which was both biodegradable and incredibly versatile.

The Algae Silk collection became an instant sensation, showcasing the potential of sustainable materials. Each garment in the collection told a story of nature and technology working in harmony. The fabric's vibrant hues and soft texture captivated fashion enthusiasts, while its environmental benefits won the hearts of eco-conscious consumers.

Isabella and Liam's partnership inspired other designers to seek out collaborations with experts in various fields. The fusion of fashion and science led to the creation of innovative materials and designs that were as functional as they were beautiful. These partnerships demonstrated that the future of fashion lay in interdisciplinary collaboration.

One of the most notable collaborations was between tech entrepreneur Ava Patel and designer Marcus Lee. Ava's expertise in wearable technology and Marcus's flair for avant-garde fashion resulted in the creation of garments that could monitor air quality and provide real-time feedback to the wearer.

This innovative collection not only raised awareness about environmental issues but also showcased the potential of tech-infused fashion.

The success of these collaborations highlighted the importance of working together to achieve common goals. By combining their unique skills and perspectives, designers and scientists could create sustainable solutions that were greater than the sum of their parts. The power of collaboration became a driving force behind the eco-tech couture movement.

7

Chapter 7: Eco-Friendly Dyeing Techniques

Traditional dyeing processes are often harmful to the environment, releasing toxic chemicals and consuming vast amounts of water. However, the fashion industry has begun to explore eco-friendly alternatives that minimize environmental impact. Innovators like Dr. Anika Mehta have developed sustainable dyeing techniques that use natural ingredients and less water.

One of Dr. Mehta's most significant breakthroughs was the development of BioDye, a dyeing process that uses bacteria to produce vibrant colors. BioDye not only reduced water consumption but also eliminated the need for harmful chemicals. The result was a range of stunning, eco-friendly fabrics that delighted designers and consumers alike.

Fashion houses around the world began to adopt BioDye, incorporating it into their collections and highlighting the environmental benefits. Designers like Zara Nguyen created garments that showcased the beautiful, natural hues produced by BioDye. These collections were celebrated for their aesthetic appeal and commitment to sustainability.

Another innovative technique was AirDye, which used air instead of water to transfer color onto fabrics. This process significantly reduced water usage and energy consumption, making it an eco-friendly alternative to traditional dyeing methods. Designers like Leo Tan embraced AirDye, creating collections that were as environmentally friendly as they were visually striking.

The adoption of eco-friendly dyeing techniques marked a significant step forward for the fashion industry. By prioritizing sustainable practices, designers could create beautiful garments without compromising the environment. These innovations demonstrated that fashion could be both stylish and sustainable, inspiring a new generation of eco-conscious designers.

8

Chapter 8: The Rise of Slow Fashion

In a world dominated by fast fashion, the slow fashion movement emerged as a response to the industry's environmental and ethical challenges. Slow fashion advocates for a more thoughtful, deliberate approach to fashion, prioritizing quality over quantity and sustainability over trends.

One of the pioneers of slow fashion was designer Nadia Rahman, who believed that clothing should be cherished and passed down through generations. Nadia's collections featured timeless designs made from sustainable materials, and each piece was crafted with meticulous attention to detail. Her work inspired consumers to invest in high-quality, durable garments that would stand the test of time.

Nadia's boutique, Evergreen Couture, became a symbol of the slow fashion movement. Her garments were made to order, ensuring that each piece was unique and tailored to the wearer's preferences. This approach not only reduced waste but also fostered a deeper connection between the consumer and their clothing.

The success of Evergreen Couture inspired other designers to adopt slow fashion principles. Workshops and educational programs were established to teach aspiring designers about sustainable practices and the importance of quality craftsmanship. The slow fashion movement gained momentum, attracting a dedicated following of consumers who valued sustainability and ethical production.

One of the most notable slow fashion initiatives was the Community Craft Project, which brought together artisans from around the world to create unique, handcrafted garments. This initiative not only promoted traditional craftsmanship but also provided economic opportunities for artisans in developing countries. The Community Craft Project showcased the potential of slow fashion to make a positive impact on both the environment and society.

As the slow fashion movement continued to grow, it became clear that consumers were eager for a more sustainable, ethical approach to fashion. Designers like Nadia Rahman and initiatives like the Community Craft Project demonstrated that fashion could be both beautiful and responsible, inspiring a global shift towards slow fashion.

9

Chapter 9: Green Fashion Capitals

As the eco-tech couture movement gained momentum, certain cities emerged as green fashion capitals, leading the charge in sustainable fashion innovation. These cities became hubs for eco-conscious designers, entrepreneurs, and consumers, fostering a culture of sustainability and creativity.

One such city was Copenhagen, which hosted the annual Copenhagen Fashion Summit. This event brought together industry leaders, policymakers, and activists to discuss the future of sustainable fashion. The summit featured runway shows, workshops, and panel discussions, highlighting the latest innovations in eco-tech couture. Copenhagen quickly became known as a global leader in sustainable fashion, attracting designers and consumers from around the world.

Another green fashion capital was Portland, Oregon, which embraced a holistic approach to sustainability. The city's vibrant eco-fashion scene was characterized by its emphasis on local production, ethical sourcing, and innovative design. Designers like Hannah O'Connor created collections that celebrated Portland's unique blend of nature and urbanity, using locally sourced materials and eco-friendly production methods.

In Asia, Tokyo emerged as a green fashion capital, with its dynamic blend of traditional craftsmanship and cutting-edge technology. The city's fashion scene was marked by its commitment to sustainability, with designers like

Yuki Nakamura leading the charge. Yuki's collections combined traditional Japanese techniques with modern, sustainable materials, creating garments that were both timeless and innovative.

These green fashion capitals not only showcased the potential of eco-tech couture but also inspired other cities to follow suit. Initiatives like green fashion weeks and sustainable design competitions were established around the world, promoting the principles of eco-friendly fashion. These events provided a platform for emerging designers to showcase their work and connect with like-minded individuals.

The rise of green fashion capitals demonstrated the global impact of the eco-tech couture movement. By fostering a culture of sustainability and innovation, these cities paved the way for a more sustainable future in fashion. The influence of green fashion capitals continued to grow, inspiring designers and consumers to embrace the principles of eco-tech couture.

10

Chapter 10: Education and Advocacy

Education and advocacy played a crucial role in the growth of the eco-tech couture movement. By raising awareness about the environmental impact of fashion and promoting sustainable practices, advocates and educators inspired a new generation of eco-conscious designers and consumers.

One of the most influential educators in this field was Professor Elena Garcia, who established the Sustainable Fashion Institute. The institute offered courses and workshops on sustainable design, eco-friendly materials, and ethical production methods. Students from around the world flocked to the institute to learn from Professor Garcia and other industry experts, gaining the knowledge and skills needed to create sustainable fashion.

Professor Garcia's work extended beyond the classroom. She collaborated with policymakers and industry leaders to develop guidelines and standards for sustainable fashion. Her advocacy efforts helped to shape regulations and policies that promoted sustainability and reduced the environmental impact of the fashion industry.

Another influential advocate was environmental activist Raj Patel, who used his platform to raise awareness about the fashion industry's impact on the planet. Raj's powerful speeches and thought-provoking campaigns highlighted the need for change and inspired consumers to make more sustainable choices. His work also encouraged brands to adopt more eco-friendly practices and prioritize sustainability in their operations.

The efforts of educators and advocates like Professor Garcia and Raj Patel had a profound impact on the fashion industry. By promoting sustainability and raising awareness, they inspired a global movement towards eco-tech couture. Their work demonstrated that education and advocacy were essential components of the journey towards a more sustainable future in fashion.

As the eco-tech couture movement continued to grow, the importance of education and advocacy became increasingly evident. Schools, universities, and organizations around the world began to offer programs and resources focused on sustainable fashion. These initiatives provided aspiring designers and consumers with the tools and knowledge needed to make a positive impact on the industry.

The journey of eco-tech couture was a testament to the power of education and advocacy. By raising awareness and promoting sustainable practices, educators and advocates paved the way for a more sustainable future in fashion. Their work inspired a new generation of designers and consumers to embrace the principles of eco-tech couture, creating a brighter, more sustainable future for the industry.

11

Chapter 11: Biodegradable Fashion

In the quest for sustainability, biodegradable fashion emerged as a groundbreaking innovation. These garments are designed to break down naturally at the end of their lifecycle, leaving minimal impact on the environment. Pioneers in this field, like eco-designer Ana Morales, sought to create clothing that was not only stylish but also kind to the planet.

Ana's breakthrough came with the development of BioWear, a collection made from biodegradable fibers sourced from plants and fungi. Each garment was designed with end-of-life in mind, ensuring that it would decompose naturally without leaving harmful residues. BioWear quickly gained popularity among eco-conscious consumers, who were drawn to the idea of fashion with a minimal environmental footprint.

One of Ana's most innovative designs was the Mushroom Dress, made from mycelium—the root structure of mushrooms. This biodegradable fabric not only had a unique texture and appearance but also offered exceptional durability. The Mushroom Dress became a symbol of the potential of biodegradable fashion, showcasing the harmony between nature and design.

Another trailblazer in biodegradable fashion was designer Luca Rossi, who created garments from biodegradable polymer blends. Luca's collections featured a range of styles, from everyday wear to haute couture, all designed to break down naturally after use. His work demonstrated that biodegradable fashion could be both versatile and elegant, appealing to a wide audience.

The rise of biodegradable fashion marked a significant shift in the industry. Designers began to prioritize materials that would have a minimal environmental impact, paving the way for a more sustainable future. The success of pioneers like Ana and Luca inspired other designers to explore biodegradable options, proving that fashion could be both innovative and eco-friendly.

12

Chapter 12: Ethical Supply Chains

Sustainability in fashion extends beyond materials and design—it also involves ethical supply chains that prioritize fair labor practices and environmental responsibility. Companies like FairFashion Collective have led the charge in promoting transparency and ethical standards in the industry.

FairFashion Collective, founded by activist and entrepreneur Amina Diallo, works with designers and manufacturers to ensure that every step of the production process meets rigorous ethical standards. From sourcing raw materials to the final garment, FairFashion Collective promotes fair wages, safe working conditions, and environmentally responsible practices.

One of FairFashion Collective's flagship initiatives was the Transparent Threads campaign, which aimed to shed light on the often opaque supply chains in the fashion industry. By providing consumers with detailed information about the origins and production of their garments, the campaign empowered them to make informed, ethical choices.

Designer Miguel Santos was one of the early adopters of the Transparent Threads campaign. His brand, Ethical Elegance, became known for its commitment to transparency and sustainability. Each garment came with a unique QR code that allowed consumers to trace its journey from raw material to finished product. This level of transparency fostered trust and accountability, setting a new standard for ethical fashion.

The movement towards ethical supply chains also included initiatives to support local artisans and small-scale producers. Brands like Artisan Threads collaborated with craftspeople from around the world, celebrating traditional techniques while ensuring fair compensation and ethical working conditions. These partnerships not only preserved cultural heritage but also promoted sustainable economic development.

The impact of ethical supply chains on the fashion industry was profound. By prioritizing fair labor practices and environmental responsibility, brands like FairFashion Collective, Ethical Elegance, and Artisan Threads demonstrated that ethical fashion could be both beautiful and principled. Their work inspired a global shift towards greater transparency and accountability in the industry.

13

Chapter 13: Fashion for a Cause

Fashion has the power to drive social change and raise awareness about critical issues. Many designers and brands have harnessed this power to create collections that support important causes and promote sustainability. One such designer is Leila Johnson, whose brand, Hope Couture, combines fashion with philanthropy.

Leila's journey began when she visited a community affected by environmental degradation. Moved by their plight, she decided to use her talents to make a difference. Hope Couture's collections are not only eco-friendly but also support various environmental and social causes. A portion of the proceeds from each collection is donated to organizations working to combat climate change, protect wildlife, and support vulnerable communities.

One of Hope Couture's most impactful initiatives was the Green Earth collection, which raised funds for reforestation projects around the world. Each garment in the collection was made from sustainable materials and featured designs inspired by nature. The collection's success not only supported reforestation efforts but also raised awareness about the importance of preserving our planet's natural resources.

Another inspiring example of fashion for a cause is the partnership between designer Aisha Malik and the nonprofit organization Clean Oceans Foundation. Together, they launched the Ocean Guardian collection, featuring garments made from recycled ocean plastics. The collection aimed to raise awareness about marine pollution and support the foundation's efforts to clean up the world's oceans.

Aisha's work extended beyond her collections. She organized beach clean-up events and educational programs to engage communities in the fight against marine pollution. Her dedication to the cause inspired others to take action and highlighted the potential of fashion to drive positive change.

Fashion for a cause has proven to be a powerful tool for raising awareness and supporting important issues. Designers like Leila Johnson and Aisha Malik have demonstrated that fashion can be a force for good, inspiring a global movement towards greater social and environmental responsibility.

14

Chapter 14: The Future of Sustainable Fashion

As the eco-tech couture movement continues to evolve, the future of sustainable fashion holds exciting possibilities. Advances in technology, materials, and design are paving the way for a more sustainable and innovative industry. Designers, scientists, and consumers alike are embracing new ideas and pushing the boundaries of what is possible.

One of the most promising areas of innovation is the development of bioengineered fabrics. Researchers are exploring the potential of lab-grown materials, such as spider silk and leather made from animal cells. These bioengineered fabrics offer the promise of sustainable, cruelty-free alternatives to traditional materials, with the potential to revolutionize the fashion industry.

Another exciting development is the rise of circular fashion models, which prioritize the reuse and recycling of garments. Companies like Loop Fashion have pioneered subscription-based services that allow consumers to rent and return clothing, reducing waste and promoting a more sustainable approach to fashion consumption.

Smart textiles are also poised to play a significant role in the future of sustainable fashion. These innovative fabrics can monitor the wearer's health, regulate body temperature, and even adapt to environmental changes.

The potential applications of smart textiles extend beyond fashion, offering solutions for healthcare, sports, and emergency services.

The future of sustainable fashion also includes a greater focus on inclusivity and accessibility. Designers are increasingly prioritizing diversity and representation in their collections, ensuring that sustainable fashion is accessible to all. Initiatives like Adaptive Couture are leading the way, creating stylish, eco-friendly garments for individuals with disabilities.

As the eco-tech couture movement continues to grow, the possibilities for sustainable fashion are endless. By embracing innovation, collaboration, and inclusivity, the fashion industry can create a brighter, more sustainable future. The journey of eco-tech couture is just beginning, and the future holds limitless potential.

15

Chapter 15: A Global Movement

The eco-tech couture movement is more than just a trend—it's a global movement that transcends borders and cultures. Designers, consumers, and activists from around the world are coming together to promote sustainability and drive positive change in the fashion industry.

One of the most inspiring aspects of this movement is the collaboration between diverse communities and cultures. From traditional artisans in rural villages to cutting-edge designers in bustling metropolises, people from all walks of life are contributing to the eco-tech couture movement. This global collaboration fosters a sense of unity and shared purpose, highlighting the power of collective action.

In Africa, designers like Nandi Okoro are blending traditional techniques with modern, sustainable practices. Nandi's brand, Heritage Threads, celebrates the rich cultural heritage of her homeland while promoting eco-friendly materials and ethical production methods. Her collections feature vibrant prints and intricate embroidery, showcasing the beauty of African craftsmanship.

In South America, designer Sofia Rivera has become a leader in the sustainable fashion movement. Her brand, EcoAndes, sources materials from local communities and uses environmentally responsible production methods. Sofia's work not only supports the local economy but also raises awareness about the importance of preserving the region's natural resources.

In Europe, the city of Amsterdam has emerged as a hub for sustainable fashion innovation. The city's EcoFashion Week attracts designers, entrepreneurs, and activists from around the world, showcasing the latest advancements in eco-tech couture. Events like these provide a platform for collaboration and inspire others to join the movement.

The global nature of the eco-tech couture movement highlights the importance of working together to create a more sustainable future. By sharing knowledge, resources, and ideas, designers and consumers can drive positive change and promote sustainability on a global scale.

As the movement continues to grow, it's clear that eco-tech couture is more than just a fashion trend—it's a global call to action. The journey towards sustainability is ongoing, and the future of fashion is in the hands of those who are willing to innovate, collaborate, and advocate for positive change.

Book Description:

In a world where fashion and environmental consciousness often seem at odds, "Eco-Tech Couture: Style Meets Sustainability" bridges the gap by exploring the harmonious fusion of style and eco-friendly innovation. This book takes readers on a journey through the revolutionary realm of sustainable fashion, where cutting-edge technology and creative design converge to create a brighter, more responsible future.

Starting with the historical context of fashion and technology's intersection, the book delves into the early pioneers who envisioned a sustainable future for couture. Readers will uncover the transformative power of materials derived from unexpected sources, such as ocean plastics and agricultural waste, and witness the rise of innovative fabrics like SeaSilk and Agraloft.

Tech-infused textiles take center stage, featuring garments that not only dazzle but also serve practical purposes like harnessing solar energy and monitoring health. The art of upcycling breathes new life into discarded items, showcasing the beauty and creativity that can emerge from fashion waste. Digital design and virtual fashion shows revolutionize the industry, reducing waste and expanding creative possibilities.

The narrative continues with the power of collaboration, highlighting partnerships between designers, scientists, and engineers that push the

CHAPTER 15: A GLOBAL MOVEMENT

boundaries of sustainable fashion. Eco-friendly dyeing techniques and the slow fashion movement are explored, emphasizing quality craftsmanship and ethical practices. The book also shines a spotlight on green fashion capitals, education, and advocacy, demonstrating the global impact of the eco-tech couture movement.

Readers will be inspired by stories of designers and brands using fashion for a cause, supporting environmental and social initiatives. The future of sustainable fashion is envisioned with bioengineered fabrics, circular fashion models, smart textiles, and a commitment to inclusivity and accessibility.

"Eco-Tech Couture: Style Meets Sustainability" is a captivating and insightful exploration of the innovative world of sustainable fashion. Through engaging stories and detailed descriptions, this book celebrates the potential of fashion to be both stylish and eco-friendly, inspiring a global movement towards a more sustainable future.

www.ingramcontent.com/pod-product-compliance
Lightning Source LLC
LaVergne TN
LVHW010443070526
838199LV00066B/6167